When God Is Your Husband

When God Is Your Husband

By Lisa Schutz

XULON PRESS

Xulon Press
2301 Lucien Way #415
Maitland, FL 32751
407.339.4217

www.xulonpress.com

Unless otherwise indicated, Scripture quotations taken from the Holy Bible, New International Version (NIV). Copyright © 1973, 1978, 1984, 2011 by Biblica, Inc.™. Used by permission. All rights reserved.

Scripture quotations taken from the Holy Bible, New Living Translation (NLT). Copyright ©1996, 2004, 2007 by Tyndale House Foundation. Used by permission of Tyndale House Publishers, Inc.

ISBN-13: 978-1-6628-3877-4

Table of Contents

Chapter 1:

Latitude/Longitude;
Where Am I Going Lord

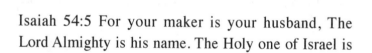

Isaiah 54:5 For your maker is your husband, The Lord Almighty is his name. The Holy one of Israel is your redeemer.

I'll never forget my ex-husband's words. It's for-ever burned into my memory like a branding of an animal, hot, painful and wounding. The four words you never expect to hear from your person, the love of your life, father of the children, and man whose last name you bear "I want a Divorce." They hit me like a lightning bolt so much so that it put me in a stage of shock and denial immediately. Oddly enough we were day two into a three day marriage strengthening seminar that he signed us up for through the USMC chaplains office. David has just returned home from a seven month deployment in May to a seven month pregnant wife graduating from college and an 18 month old son. In July we welcomed our baby girl and by October he was gone. I knew there were many things about my husband's lifestyle choices but what I didn't know was in his heart he had left long ago and had no concern for his young bride or the betterment of his young family. Through the course of many months of prayer and fasting and crying out to God he started to reveal many things to be in dreams. Different spirits that had strongholds on our marriage. Leviathan's very real grip on our house was so destructive it was absolutely determined to demolish any and all traces of the covenant we made to one another and any hope of the future for us. Nevertheless I persisted in spiritual warfare that brought me to a place of complete mental torment that led me to suicidal thoughts and such a despair that after many confirmations of the church I attended in NC and my old church family in MD that

I knew "I had to get out of there." So within a month I started packing up my home, giving away everything the Lord told me to let go of. Material possessions, all my furniture, clothing, jewelry, household items, shoes, computers, art, anything that was attached to my life with him. God started a purging process at that very moment because he knew we would end up in Divorce despite what my heart wanted. Night after night I cried out to the Lord "Where am I going, how could you, why is this happening, what did I do to deserve this." I was so angry, hurt, frustrated, confused, stripped, tired, and barren. All my dreams, hopes, plans for the future, southern living, and country lifestyle I had in my mind were destroyed and I absolutely despised the thoughts of going back to Baltimore even when I knew it was most likely where I was going. Lucky Me, I ended up in a mildewed, cold, wet basement. By the way, there were two bedrooms empty and completely vacant for 20+ years upstairs that we were unwelcome to. Talk about a heart-break hotel. My kids and I went from our colorful 3bd 2 bath home in the heart of NC to a prison cell in the basement of a less than hospitable family member. Back home it was. Baltimore the "heroin" capital of

America, "Murderland" the place I was so desperate to leave and never return home to. The Lord sent me back with a message of Hope, restoration, double portion and mercy, that I couldn't bare at the time. Job said it best "Though you slay me yet I will trust you Lord."

Challenge 1: Reflect on those who have caused deep pain and betrayal in your life. Maybe a previous relationship, friendship, family member or even a parent. Write out a prayer to release that pain and ask The Lord to help you heal from the trauma. Take a few minutes to let his love guide you into the process of forgiveness and the will to release them from your soul.

Chapter 2:

Faith Walk

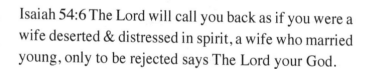

Isaiah 54:6 The Lord will call you back as if you were a wife deserted & distressed in spirit, a wife who married young, only to be rejected says The Lord your God.

I had been through months of interviews with Commanding Officers, family readiness officers, legal personnel and in between with the USMC. I had to take drastic measures to get the final fee to return home. I had painted some projects for the church I was attending at the time just to come up with $500 to have a tow hitch attached to my 4 cylinder 2012 Nissan Rogue. Two women from the church one suffered from divorce and spiritual warfare from her ex husband and a worship leader to come help me load what was left of my life there to tow 300 miles back to MD on my own with two small babies and one of 3 animals. My soon to be ex husband watched me pack everything including our children and didn't even try to stop us, fight for us, there was no remorse, no sorry, no regret, just a cold shoulder and very hard heart. It completely shattered mine. As I drove down the driveway of our home I was so hurt to look back and see everything we worked for torn to pieces and lost to the devil himself. God whispered in my ear "It's just a house, you will have better and more." Just three days after I went back to Baltimore, David had his mistress, his mother and sister all who hated me move into our home, our children's rooms and the family quarters that were mine. The anger and vengeance I had in my heart was so strong I could have killed him. It was beyond comprehension. As I went back to church in Maryland, people thought they had seen a ghost knowing how I broke free from the life and environment that I had lived prior to marriage. I started to take my place at our altar at church Sunday after Sunday desperate for a miracle of the restoration of my marriage, desperate to be healed from the bitterness and agony that crippled me, desperate to be a whole family again because the bitter realities of the hardships of single mothers was crushing. Debt was crushing, orphan/bastard children were crushing, infidelity was crushing, watching the man I loved turn into a weak, drunken, adulterous coward was crushing. The abandonment, gripped, consumed, confused, trapped and poisoned me all at once. No word could comfort, no pastor/prophet could heal my weary soul. It was only God's love, compassion, provision, grace and mercy that met me week after week, month after month and year after year to bind up the wounds of my broken heart. In the process of it all I went through multiple moves, multiple jobs, multiple obstacles with Social Services, little to no help financially when their father got out to the USMC the child support was and still is next to nothing. Nevertheless, I persisted. All the while the Lord was trading my ashes in for beauty and my trials into triumphs. I was being called forth. The battles were my training, the pain was a catalyst for forward movement. The prayers and maturation for destiny, character development, spiritual steadiness, long suffering, and trevail to be used for growth of the Woman of God he was calling me to become. The Lord himself was taking me through a faith season. Can I trust him, will I trust him, Can and will I obey him like a wife? Will I forsake him in the trenches when I blessed him in the open heavens. Will I take up my cross and press on to the mark of the call of God? It was all up to me to decide. The Lord binds up the broken hearted. He is near to those with open wounds.

Challenge 2: James 2:14 Says "Faith without works is dead." Sometimes we dont even know what to do in certain situations. This requires a faith and trust in The Lord to lead and guide us even when we cannot see or even know where we are going. Like invisible stepping stones we just have to trust him the next stone is already there, all we have to do is step.

Ask The Lord today "Lord show me the way, give me the steps and I will follow."

Take some quiet time to journal and ask The Lord to open up your ears to hear when he replies and open up your eyes to see when he shows you. Write down what you hear or see.

Chapter 3:

Sanctification

―――――――⸎―――――――

"The Lord bless you daughter" exclaimed Boaz "You are showing even more family loyalty now than ever before, for you have not gone after a young man whether rich or poor. Ruth 3:10

Celibacy, my God was this such a hard thing to gain control in a whirlwind of emotion. I went into a complete consecration before the Lord even while I was still married to David. I knew it was like playing with fire sleeping with an unfaithful spouse. Talk about longing and loneliness. Laying in bed alone night after night after knowing the comforts of one man for many years. No one to love on, depend on, or just feel the warmth of. Winter nights with no one to bear the cold, summer days with no one to adventure with. I grew tiresome of the emptiness I felt. Thank God for the altar women God put in my path to demonstrate Godly conduct, purity, godliness, holiness, integrity, prayerfulness and endurance. They knew all too well the sting of the stamp of "one" and yet they dedicated themselves to their relationships to the Lord as first and foremost. They prayed for me regularly and made it a point to challenge me to the truth "The Lord is your husband", lover of your soul and you are his beloved bride. The affection he has for you is incomparable to any earthly relationship, even a real marriage to a Godly man. Getting this reality engrafted into my spirit took much alone time with just me and him, his supernatural provisions and help and studying various chapters of scriptures on marriage, singleness, Proverbs 31, Esther, Ruth, Deborah and women of integrity used by God in the role of a "wife". My alone time also helped me to get into journalizing qualities and attributes of a Godly husband and studying the very nature of Jesus and his love for the church, Boaz and his protection and provisions for Ruth, Hosea and his unconditional love for Gomer. But in my mind there was no better romantic love story for me than Boaz and Ruth. Because Boaz took on the very nature of Christ, taking his people into a glorious marriage through salvation. He washes his bride, grants her full access to his kingdom and treasures, pays her debts, and loves her despite her lack and desolation. He calls her his very own and puts her on display & recognizing her as a quality woman to everyone he knew. Boaz was also a very wealthy landowner, Ruth was a young poor widow with nothing left in her but a strong work ethic and a fierce loyalty to her late husband's mother. God favored her for her sacrifices and purity so when she met Boaz he acted as Christ towards her. He accepted her poverty, saw her worth and instead of rejecting her he made her a jewel in his crown. She got back everything she lost and then some. Boaz and Ruth carried such seeds of destiny that she was able to birth not only King David through her lineage but the King of the World, our Lord and Savior Jesus Christ. That's redemption at its finest. Sacrifice and obedience birthed such great blessings to not only herself but the entire world! Wow! Because of my own personal sanctification process God was able to heal, restore, transform, grow, change and birth destiny within myself as well. The fullness of the manifestation of promises will be a continued choice of obedience to him.

Challenge 3: Write down the qualities you possess that will align with your call and what you value you about yourself. Thank him for such qualities and be in total surrender for those things to expand and sharpen.

Chapter 4:

Orpha Alternative

So I counsel younger widows to marry, to have children, to manage their homes and to give the enemy no opportunity for slander. Some have in fact already turned away to follow Satan. 1 Timothy 5:14-15

The results of my homecoming could have been a horror story amongst the devastation. What I was before salvation was absolutely monstrous. See prior to marriage I was a drug abuser, toxic, intoxified, untamed, violent and lustful. I started my battle with substance abuse at 12 years old. Smoking cigarettes, engaging in very inappropriate sexual circumstances, and eventually by 13, I had lost my virginity and was smoking Marijuanna on a daily basis. By 16 years old I was dancing (not ballet) wild, dating drug dealers, becoming a drug dealer and just absolutely rebellious and defiant to anything Godly. By 19 I had two domestic violence charges, assault charges, and possession charges. 2011 I hit a crossroad. I was tired of my long standing drug use, my weight was dropping, I didn't recognize myself in the mirror and I was tired. I started crying out to The Lord. I knew he was very real because of the encounters I had as a child being in revival at the same church I had returned to. I started asking God to be married, to become a mother, to be sober, to be restored. I knew I couldn't do it on my own. It had to be through him. Then a series of very unfortunate events took place to bring me to a place of true repentance and being disgusted with my life. By God's grace he saved and delivered me from every demonic attachment, possession and oppression. But coming back into this area that I had been delivered from could have sucked me right back into my old ways, my old life, my old self. I could have become Orpha. In the book of Ruth, her story was a woman of virtue who remained pure and

God honoring. However, there was another woman named Orpha in the story who chose the ladder. She was also a widow, she could have chosen to go ahead with Ruth and her mother-in-law to her deceased husband. She could have received the truth and salvation of Christ and had a godly lineage through her womb as well. However, she turned back, turned away from the promise, went back to her old desires and lustful ways. Eventually she started sleeping with many men, strange men, and her womb produced the mutated child Goliath. The very giant, Ruth's grandchild had to slay before The Lord. I can only imagine what life would have been like if I wouldn't have held fast to what I knew was true, grounded myself in the Lord, got into service ministries, Got under a great house full of rich knowledge and submitted myself to his will for my life. I could have been like Orpha went back to what I knew, went back to my old ways, let the old man's nature take over, succumbed to the devil's path for my life and gave birth to a giant. Thank God for his sovereignty. He saw it fit despite my pain to put me back on his wheel and heal me.

Challenge 4: Psalm 51:10-12 Create in me a clean heart and renew a right spirit within me.

Write out some things you know you personally struggle with that could hinder your relationship with The Lord. Ask him to cleanse you of all iniquities so he can form you into the woman he created you to become. Tell him why you see yourself in a negative way at times. Worship at his feet for a good 30mins. Allow him to love on you.

Chapter 5:

My Beloved

Set me as a seal upon your heart. as a seal upon your arm, for love is strong as death, jealousy[a] is fierce as the grave.[b]
Its flashes are flashes of fire the very flame of the LORD.
Many waters cannot quench love, neither can the floods drown it.
If a man offered for love all the wealth of his house, He would be utterly despised.

Multiple times numerous women had given me the statement "The Lord is your husband." It didn't quite resonate the first 50 times. But as I got deeper into the word and watched the very hand of God move on my behalf like a husband to provide and protect it, set it. God has done a multitude of tangible miracles on my behalf to show himself to be the very thing I couldn't wrap my mind around a "husband". The love I have for the Lord is like no other. I am 100% infatuated with the Lord. His very presence in my life is irreplaceable, the mercy I have received from him when I was so undeserving is nothing no man or woman on this Earth has ever shown me. The way he cleaned up my messes day after day, week after week, year after year was nothing short of unconditional burning love for me and I for him. I was entangled in deep spiritual warfare that tried to destroy me and my children. I couldn't see or feel a way out. So bombarded by bills, debts, children, working, loneliness, isolation, fatigue, disorientation, confusion and utter disgrace with my life. I couldn't do anything but rely on the Lord. I didn't have a choice. Through the course of 3 long years the Lord Showed up for me in many ways I would have never imagined. But especially in the area of finances. Times where I had no idea how we could afford anything. He made a way, big things like debt cancellations, new cars in the midst of repossessions the same day, having a single-family house, great paying jobs, all sorts of things. I have been mind-blown by God over and over again. I don't know how I would have made it without him. I wouldn't have. I did have a part to play in my obedience to the Lord, The Prophet who I sat under, and being in subjection to handling God's business. For that he multiplied my hands every time and built a strong faith in the process of it all. I gave him all I had, everything in me. My time, my finances, my emotions, my prayers and longings, my desires, my life. I was in love, with the lover of my soul. I was in love with the only one who could heal, restore, recreate, replenish, resurrect, direct, revive, resuscitate, and restore my life. He was the hand guiding me through all the bad, blessed in the midst, sending those who had pure intentions to help me, strengthen me and get my back to a place where I could stand again. He is the one for me, my everything. I could never turn my back on him now. Not even when I came to this place of meeting a new beloved. The man I thought was my husband to be, who was not.

Challenge 5: Study the attributes of a husband biblically. In Corinthians, Ruth, and even Proverbs 31. Study the scriptures of the characteristics of love. This is the very nature and heart of Christ and his unconditional love. It never fails. Write down these attributes so you can use them in a guide to all your personal relationships.

Chapter 6:

First Love After Divorce

———— ⌒⌒⌒⌒ ————

"Above All Things have fervent charity amongst yourselves, for charity shall cover a multitude of sins."
1 Peter 4:8

Much of my time alone I cried out to God for a godly husband. Much of my time there was confirmation from the Holy Spirit he was coming and close. Nine long months I kept hearing it louder and louder in my spirit "Boaz". I dreamed of what he would be like, made lists of the attributes I was looking for. I always knew I wanted someone with grit, who could understand my messy background, someone with business savvy because I knew we would be doing both business and ministry together. Someone with intelligence and poise, a great dresser, a man of prayer and someone who knew the word well. I waited so long. As I sat on my bed one night I was in the book of Ruth and I had it open. Annoyed with my circumstance of loneliness I kind of commanded God "I have been in this book for 9 months now, if you are going to do it then just DO IT." The very next morning at 7am I received such an unexpected personal message on my Facebook. It was from an old friend that I never expected to hear from again. I laughed and thought to myself "No way Lord" my friend from high school was someone who I had to let go of when his personal feelings for me were unreciprocated. He had just finished an 8-year prison sentence and had come home divorced, but hidden and restored in God's grace and the one I thought I had been waiting for. When I saw him again for the first time in person I was immediately head over heels. We had already been speaking for days on the phone previously and I knew he knew the word. He spoke to me in parables and psalms. So poetic and charming. We connected in a way I had never known before and we grew super close super fast. I went to pick him up for a Thursday night bible study and when he came out to my car one look with those bright green eyes, one smell of his scented oils, and one big dumb cheese smile from both of us and that was it for me. It was him. I was sold in every way. My pastors included could see God in and all over him. He knew he was called, he knew he was released for a purpose to be a regional evangelist and voice. I wanted to see all of his capabilities in action. How much he could do with his anointing. We were the same in many ways. We communicated with just looks, we bonded through scripture, emotion, art, and music. Sometimes being too much alike can lead to many debates as well. I didn't care though, I love him purely and wholeheartedly. Many warnings started to arise however. The realities of a young man just released from prison and back into the world and all its temptations eventually started to take a toll on him and us. Not to mention some of the character flaws we both needed to adjust. I started to realize he was going down a bad path and consequently so did I with it. The man who leads your home is the most crucial decision you could ever make. While I to this day reflect on what if it were different, there are things that have to be in proper order before that could ever really bear lasting roots. We started sleeping together, he was at my house so much it was as if we lived together, we were disobeying God and bore the consequences. My love continued on to develop a drinking habit and is now a recreational marijuanna smoker again. The old man was rising up once more trying to squeeze God out of him. Spiritual warfare at its finest. One night he was staying with me and God woke me up at 4 in the morning, he spoke to me and said you cannot go any further with him. The drinking and smoking will not be your portion. I knew what he was saying, it was time to let go. It was the most painful reality I had felt in quite some time. I woke my man up and told him God was speaking to me and he had to make a decision. When he got up that day he left my house for a party, and made his choice. I knew it was going to be different between us at that point. And it was. Nevertheless, I still wanted him, and as much as I wish it could have been different, I wanted my God more.

Challenge 6: Examine a time you disobeyed God and he gave you multiple chances to listen. How did it go? What lessons would you learn from it? How did you grow?

Chapter 7:

Unfaithful Woman, Faithful God

When The Lord began to speak to Hosea "Go marry a promiscuous woman and have children with her, for like an adulterous wife, this land is guilty of unfaithfulness to The Lord." Hosea 1:1-2

There were days that God really dealt with my sin and I was constantly scared of losing the Holy Spirit. Many times God literally covered his face from my sin where shown to me prophetically. It truly used to break my heart. Every time I laid with this man such guilt and shame would come over me. It wasn't that

God hated me for my sins but that he knew what was about to come upon me. Wickedness, pain, anguish and darkness. He also knew I was idolizing this man and making him God. He also knew I was giving the devil full access to my mind, body and soul and it was decaying me little by little. One night when we started getting intimate with each other, I was woken out of my sleep with the feeling of a chain around my neck. I was literally choking and gagging and I felt like I was being pulled by the neck with this chain. I was led into my apartment bathroom and I sat in my tub and cried out to The Lord for his forgiveness. There was a literal demonic presence in my house torturing me. Because of the magnitude of sin from the purity I was letting go of, I brought a Jezebel spirit right into my life and she is a wicked, nasty snake. Another time right in the middle of being intimate he heard literal hissing in his ear. We both had to stop and repent and he told that thing to bow. However, his authority was void because we gave it legal access to be there. I can recall many times crying after sex with him. Many times crying out to God for forgiveness and telling this man a thousand times if we want to be together we have to get married, but it never happened. Later however, I realized what the enemy meant for evil God can always use for his glory and brought me to Hosea's story of God's unconditional Mercy, love and empathy for humanity triumphs over sin.

Hosea married a prostitute named Gomer. Their story was one one of hardship and tragedy but later led to redemption. Gomer was always sleeping around with other men, leaving her husband as a charlot. One day she was so far gone she ended up in sex slave trade. Hosea had to go and find his wife and buy her back just to show his love for her and display God's faithfulness to the unfaithful. True unconditional love. See despite our shortcomings and unfaithfulness he will still redeem us, chase us down, and speak softly to return home. Even in the midst of my sin even after knowing God to be my husband and making that vow. Even after I crossed the line and fell into the trap Satan was planting for me, even while I was in that unfaithful circumstance he loved me enough to continue to pursue me, forgive me, replenish me, heal me and remind me I was his. That his love for me was jealous and I was better off just me and him. Despite my willfulness to stay in an adulterous relationship (a sexual relationship outside of the context of marriage) he chasented me, wooed me back into his guidance. Offered me support and Jesus pleaded the blood at the right hand of The Father on my behalf.

Challenge 7: Repent for former adulterous relationships (if this applies) and ask God to grant the same pardon for your sins. To wash you clean and put a new garment of praise on you.

Chapter 8:

Now Faith

Now to the one who works, wages are not credited as a gift but as an obligation. However, to the one who does not work but trusts God who justifies the ungodly, their faith is credited as righteousness. David said the same thing when he said "Blessed are those whose transgressions are forgiven, whose sins are covered. Blessed is the one whose sin the Lord will never count against them." Romans 4:1-8

In the midst of this nine month endeavour The Lord continued to bless and favor me. There were some extremely hard choices I had to make, some new doors I had to walk through. Some doors I had to close, pages I had to turn, projects I had to start and finish and I wasn't sure if it were still possible to ask for those things in the midst of deep sinfulness. My church didn't really approve of him and I anymore. They knew we were in sin and by being so they reprimanded me harshly and it was so confusing. I knew God was calling me out of a full-time job and into my business but my leadership also believed it was a poor choice because past circumstances had proven so. I was doubting my own worth and value in the church because of my complex dynamic and abilities that didn't seem to be fitting the mold any longer. My man had pointed out some really truthful and biblical points about the church as a whole I wasn't ready to receive and it was very difficult to grasp it all at the same time. I was constantly in a meeting with someone to help "guide my life" which was fine, it was what I was used to and truthfully something I needed in years past but I knew God was speaking things contrary to their advice and opinions. All at once I stepped out of my church, quit my job and pursued this relationship with this person who I was already in sin with and I was scared out of my mind. But I had faith in my God to see me through no matter what the consequences. And he did. When I left my job, I had already had notebooks full of ideas of how to capitalize on my skill sets and abilities in the beauty and business industry. I had a business plan for a trade school for initial beauty but also many other skills. I had gotten my Microblading Certification just a few months prior and I heard the Holy Spirit so clearly, launch the school for Microblading. So, I put together a curriculum, agenda, tools, and all the supplies for students started to market my services and within a month I had 4 people sign up for my 8-hour 1 day training at the Best Western Plus downtown. In total after all expenses were paid, I made $3200.00 that day. Enough to pay all my bills. Since then I have successfully trained 5 students in Microblading and 1 student in Lash Extensions. Favor. When I left my church, I was heart-broken. It was my safety net, my family, and my crutch all at the same time. I longed for more, I longed to be with young prophets, apostles, marketplace ministers, and evangelists really doing great things for God. Nomads that converged for his glory and purposes. It wasn't long after I left my home church the Holy Spirit pointed me to a young prophet/apostle out in New Jersey who was affiliated with them. He was who I needed to align with for sure. Him and his wife and their giftings and callings were exactly what I knew I was looking for. I had been asking God to "establish me in the company of the Prophets" for a while and I knew I needed more training in traveling, prophecy, visions, signs, wonders, miracles, and supernatural healings. Another answered prayer and door opened for a sinful daughter rebelling at the time. Over the course of the next few months my Prophet of Nations call had been confirmed multiple times. That was a miracle to me in of itself because no one in my church ever even dared try to help me with that gift or mantle even though I knew I was different and that is why I was under such an attack all the time. When you have a prophetic call or anointing or mantle the warfare grows stronger to make and try to break you. God purposes it all together to get the glory. Shortly after all of that however I noticed my spiritual vigor and fervancy was dying out a little and it took me to travel out of state and be in prophetic atmospheres to give me my boost to keep moving forward in faith. God continued blessing me, kept loving on me, kept speaking to me, kept dealing with me and still answered multiple prayers and opened multiple doors for my good and success. I knew I wanted to start seeing more tangible miracles in healings and breakthroughs in prayers for others so God was allowing those things as well. I had gone to Jersey one Sunday to go to the prophet's church and after an impartation I came home and I stopped at the local gas station down the street from me. There was a girl in there who was wearing a wrist band and complaining of her wrist being tight and fractured. I asked if I could pray for her and instantly I could feel the power of God rushing through my hands with heat and she was healed. No more issues to this day. Another example of God's awe working wonder in the Earth through a life of faith. I had seen and operated in healing before but not so instant and precise.

Challenge 8: Can you recall a time you ever felt like an outsider? Misunderstood or misguided? Write a few descriptive words that define those emotions. (Ex. Alone, Forgotten)

Now write out what God says about you instead. (Ex. Called, Chosen)

Chapter 9:

Hagerstown, really?

———— ❦ ————

Deuteronomy 6:11 "I will give you houses filled with all kinds of good things you did not provide, wells you did not dig, and vineyards and olive groves you did not plant—then when you eat and are satisfied."

B ack Track, I always knew Baltimore was a temporary thing, and it was confirmed in my spirit as well as by one other person who has been walking with me since I came back to Baltimore. Someone I trusted and knew every intimate detail of what I was going through. She was also very prophetic and under the radar. When I was praying and fasting in NC, I kept asking God ultimately where I was going. I knew Baltimore was for sure but I was still very unsettled about it because I knew I didn't want to remain there. One morning I woke up from a deep sleep and I heard it as clear as someone sitting next to me "Hagerstown". I had no idea what that meant because I had never been there, I wasn't expecting that answer and I was baffled by it. But all the years that I remained in Baltimore housing access was always denied. Things were never really built on solid ground and things were always shifting. I was so determined to come check this area out in the year 2017 I called my dad and we came out for the day. I also applied to spas, applied for housing, found a church that I researched and tried to figure out a way to get here. It wasn't the time yet however so I let it go. During all these years Prophets spoke of the saints of God moving to new cities and regions for God's plans and purposes. The scripture above was constantly being prophesied out of my mouth for my own personal life. The two main things I truly wanted, personal desires of my heart were to be remarried and settle back into a beautiful piece of land in a country atmosphere with that man. One cold night at the tail end of 2019 after my breakup and all my transitions I was in a Denny's with my mentor, she and I were discussing my direction in life. She and I both knew I wanted change and I was ready for a New Beginning. While we were eating and talking she had a vision of a rural area with farm and land. She said I would run rehabilitation housing and ministries for the broken (which I already knew) with my husband who would serve with me in this vision. I knew instantly the vision was of Hagerstown. What I didn't know was how and when this would all transpire. I knew I had to purpose it in my spirit however to start the process of looking at the area again and really seeking the Lord's counsel on it. December 2019 I started to reconnect with an old friend from middle school Allen Ray Jackson. He was in a transition period time of his life as well. Tired of living a street life, fast life, drug abuse and longing for answers. He was crying out to God for years. I had been evangelising to him a while before I met my ex. But he was in a toxic relationship and wasn't able to have a friendship with me at the time. So he reached back out to me a year later and wanted to catch up. I knew instantly God was calling me to pray for him to receive salvation and pursue a life in Christ through baptism. We got close and he was healing from our friendship. January 8, 2020, my Father Vernon Allen Schutz traumatically passed away of a heart attack. We were not expecting or anticipating his untimely death. The morning he passed Allen had heard something (God) tell him not to go to work that day, so he took off. I texted him to let him know what happened and he was broken with me. He had previously lost his younger brother to overdose a few years prior and understood the sting of death. Allen reminded me of my dad so much. The smoking, the risky behavior but also kind eyes, witty banter, strong intuition and drawn to the supernatural. It broke my heart to watch him self-destruct and rebel against God. I know that's what brought my father to an early grave. So after a lot of prayer, a lot of tug of war with his pride, a few kicks in the butt, and a lot of grace I got Allen to pray the sinner's prayer and get baptised at this pool club I was working for at the time. I knew he had to go to church to stay rooted and I knew he needed further deliverance. One day The Lord spoke to me and said "Take him to that church in Hagerstown." So I did. As I was driving back home God started to speak to me again. "This is

your home and your husband and you will live here."
I wondered if Allen was it, but The Lord confirmed
he was not. That was painful as well. Allen had only
ever shown me genuine care, affection, and love. He
never wanted anything in return but those attributes and
wanted to be with me. He truly reminded me what genuine friendship, care and concern from a man looked
like. I hadn't had it in a long time. He never compared
me, disrespected me, put me aside, turned his back or
abandoned me. It hurt when I realized I had to let him
go. He is a genuine person with many loving qualities.
I cherish our friendship to this day.

Challenge 9: Can you recall a time The Lord sent true
companionship your way to heal and restore you? Write
them a letter to thank them for their faithfulness to you.
Pray for their safety and protection.

Chapter 10:

Laid Up For The Just

A good man leaves an inheritance for his children's children, but the wealth of the wicked is laid up for the righteous. Proverbs 13:22

L et's talk about my father now. My father was a Military man. Born and raised in Baltimore. Got to travel all over, served many years in the Air Force, Air National Guard and other DOD platforms. After he too lost his younger brother, father and step father he developed issues of alcohol addiction, smoking, drug abuse and living a life of his own pleasures. Never truly devoting himself to anything or anyone with his whole heart. While he and my mother were married many years and never separated she always had to find herself sacrificing who she was for his own usual selfish desires. I won't bad mouth my father because not all of him was bad. However his monies were never really centered towards the family or The Lord. Frequently it was gambled, spent haphazardly, recreationally, on bars, food, and all the sins of debauchery. The Lord has shown me the error in those ways. The Lord has also had me prophecy many years about "The Great Transfer of Wealth" from the unjust to the just. To the ones who don't steward God's resources properly to those who do and will for his glory and purposes. The Lord often showed me that I would carry wealth and increase because I am willing to do his will. While I still have a long way to go before I can properly steward millions, I do believe he will allow that kind of provision to flow through my hands. My father has many pensions, streams of income, and monies laid up for his service years. But as I had stated he didn't steward them properly. My mother suffered poverty and shambles for many years under his leadership. As much as he had they lived in complete squallor. Such a shame. I couldn't even walk into my family home without complete devastation in my spirit. Conditions that are more underkept then some housing in the City of Baltimore. Although it pains me that I won't be able to see my father enjoy his life, health or money anymore I do believe it's a grace The Lord allowed in his passing to transfer my father's hidden wealth and pull myself and my mother out of such impoverished conditions. We otherwise would still both be in our frustrating circumstances of lack and survival. My mother, while learning, still has a poverty mentality and spirit and God will have to heal and break that to her good. God is starting a new chapter for us in 2020 to declare his word never comes back void, that he keeps his promises even in the midst of our inability to be perfect, to show himself mighty on our behalf, to slay the crooked serpent Leviathan right in front of our very eyes. To show tangible signs, wonders and miracles. That he can and will bring the wall of Jericho down and to allow us to Pass/Crossover from the wilderness to our Canaan. To release our inheritance to us and allow us to obtain our lands and possessions. That The Lord will establish us and the works of our hands, and allow our lines to fall in pleasant places. That's the kind of God I serve. A true love, the only one who can do such awestruck wonders on our behalf. We are literally going from the PIT to the PALACE like Joesph or Esther.

Challenge 10: What are you believing God for? Are you preparing to receive those blessings? Write down what you believe his promises are to you and how you know he will fulfill them.

Chapter 11:

Believe The Prophets

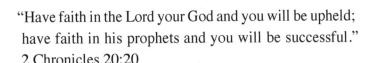

"Have faith in the Lord your God and you will be upheld; have faith in his prophets and you will be successful." 2 Chronicles 20:20

Throughout the course of these 4 years now I have been to many conferences, church services, prophetic meetings, online seminars, spiritual gatherings and 100s of hours of prayer time. And the same theme has always proven itself to be meaningful. LISTEN TO THE PROPHETS. Prophets are the mouthpieces of the heart and mind of the Lord. They see, hear, speak and declare more accurately than any other human being to walk this planet. They are chosen from the beginning of time to be extra special in the sight of The Lord. The Lord says he will not do ANYTHING on the Earth without FIRST telling his friends the Prophets. That means he has a deep relationship with these humans and they are devout before him. Constantly. I took on that understanding and when the Prophets declared blessing, I always sowed into their ministries. When they declared open doors, I took it seriously and I always saw the result of their declaration, when they declare healing and power it never fails people start getting healed, power of God breaks out, lives are changed, things are transformed and his will is carried out on the Earth. Prophets have blessed my business, spoken into my own prophetic mantle and call, decreed healing in my home, shared visions and dreams, imparted the sound of heaven into my giftings, art into my world and have always confirmed what God has spoken over my life personally.

Matthew 10:41 "Whoever welcomes a Prophet as a Prophet will receive a Prophet's reward."

It reminds me of the story in 2 Kings 7:3-20. The Prophet Elijah prophesied that the famine in the land would come to an end and the city would again prosper and be wealthy. The King of the city at that time was in disbelief and was unable to receive the word of The Lord and therefore was unable to receive the blessings. Some people hear the Prophets or Kingdom leaders and have no regard and therefore cannot partake of the supernatural benefits. On the other hand there were lepers broken, hungry and diseased with no other options other than to move forward and trust God. They came upon a city of the Syrians who were tyrants of the land of that time. They could stay where they were and die or they could move forward by faith and hope to receive food. Since they chose faith God blessed them. They walked into a city and found it abandoned with all good things and partook of Kingdom blessings. Food, silver, gold, wheat, wine, (provision and blessings) he also protected them because they thought they would surely die from the famine or an enslavement of the Syrians. There were many times where I didn't have any other choice but to trust my husband and partake of his goodness when I couldn't fend for myself. I sowed and it was multiplied, I prayed and received, I served and survived the devour the enemy was trying to bring into my camp. Since I believe The Lord and listen to his prophets I constantly receive their rewards and kingdom privileges. Amen to That.

Challenge 11: Do you have a spiritual leader or prophetic guide? Sow a seed of faith into their ministry asking God to increase it supernaturally. You won't be disappointed.

Chapter 12:

The Widow and The Oil

Elisha replied to her, "How can I help you? Tell me, what do you have in your house?" Your servant has nothing there at all," she said, "except a small jar of olive oil." Elisha said, "Go around and ask all your neighbors for empty jars. Don't ask for just a few. Then go inside and shut the door behind you and your sons. Pour oil into all the jars, and as each is filled, put it to one side." She left him and shut the door behind her and her sons. They brought the jars to her and she kept pouring. When all the jars were full, she said to her son, "Bring me another one." But he replied, "There is not a jar left." Then the oil stopped flowing. She went and told the man of God, and he said, "Go, sell the oil and pay your debts. You and your sons can live on what is left."

It finally happened, after four years of prophecy, intercession, standing, doubting, believing, declaring, receiving words of affirmation and standing on promises, a wealth transfer finally came to pass. This scripture was highlighted to me on MULTIPLE occasions. Multiple people had described me as the widow with the oil. My Ex, prophetic people, intercessors, and God himself over and over had me study this scripture. God's word came to pass, when it's God his word never lies and it never comes back void. For four years, I kept hearing the number $175,000.00 in my spirit. That it would all come together full circle, I didn't know how or when but I wrote that number down almost 100xs and wrote out what I would do with it. EVERY SINGLE TIME. December 2019 it started to happen. I had a small storage container broken into with a lot of old things but family things, clothes, household items etc. At the time I was very upset not realizing it was part of a divine set up. After filing a police report, I made a detailed list and then filed a claim with my insurance company. I was only expecting to get back maybe a thousand or two, low and behold I received back almost six thousand dollars in appraisals. So I got to invest into my business, pay up some bills, bless my family with a great Christmas like we've never had before and be at peace with myself for the next month or two. Then, at tax time, I received up to $9,000 in returns. Therefore also, restoring things back into my business, paying off some debts, sowing back into the kingdom and preparing myself for the next season. It also helped cover some of my Father's funeral expenses. Then my Father passed away. At first my mother had believed we wouldn't be receiving anything from all of his years in the military. I knew that just wasn't true. But my Father was a very private man and did not extend his personal or financial matters to anyone, not even my Mother. So it took petitioning the Courts of Heaven (a very real place) to have some kind of statement, or phone call released. After a month we got it, his life insurance money of $95,000.00. We also received a couple thousand dollars back from various financial associations that he had previously done business with. Then we got our last lump sum of money for the sale of my childhood home of $60,000.00. Between all those monies it came out to around $180,000.00. WOW. God's all working wonders manifesting right before our eyes. It pains me to have to lose my Father and yet I know it was all part of his plan. My Father made it to Heaven this I know. He suffers no more with addiction, identity, selfishness, unwholesomeness and battle. I know he made it because it's been confirmed by the Judge himself. We will live on this inheritance for years to come.

(Please remember these are coming from a SINGLE MOTHER of TWO on h own in a poverty situation)

Tangible Miracles/Favor/Gifts Documented from 2016-2020

1. No money or occupation to return home with. The Lord had a church in NC hire me to paint for them and had the exact amount to cover moving expenses, to the penny amount.

2. Obtaining one of the most reputable lawyers in Maryland to do litigations for me in my divorce for just $1,000.00 after the lawyer I originally wanted to hire was hired by my ex husband.

That lawyer charged him thousands of dollars for his services.

3. Multiple great paying jobs with potentials to make bonuses, commissions and benefits. (Management Positions, Beauty School Instructor, Sales and CSR for #1 Flooring distribution on the East Coast, MedSpa Aesthetician and Spa Coordinator)

4. Being able to afford my own single family home on my own for rent for a year. God opened up a great job and that home after prayer and fasting.

5. Local Military Credit union cutting my debt in half from $30,000 to $15,000 and settling out my debt as is.

6. Purchasing a brand new car the same day my current car was being repossessed.

7. Leaving my job to start my school in 2 weeks making $3,800.00

8. A local bank in NC cancelled a total debt of $1,000 in my favor

9. I had prayed for YEARS for a King sized bed and new furniture after I gave mine away to a local girls home, a brand NEW King Set,

Entertainment stand and sectional couch was given to me 3 years later.

10. Multiple times where my rent was due and in 24 hours I had come up with $1,000 through various services.

11. Multiple times where I didn't think I had enough to cover my expenses and unknown monies would come out of nowhere.

12. Multiple times where specific people God used would say to me "The Lord had me give this to you" and hand me money to cover expenses.

13. Multiple times of believing in double portions and receiving double portions.

14. $15,000.00 released to me in two months

15. My Fathers passing releasing $160,000.00 into our hands

16. Purchasing a beautiful new home in Hagerstown MD

17. Purchasing two new cars in the same day

Challenge 12: Write out a number that you think could benefit you and God to bless your house and others. Write out how you would spend it and what you would contribute it to. See what The Lord says back.

Prayers that produce blessings

1. Prayer of Jabez: 1 Chronicles 4:10

And Jabez called on the God of Israel, saying, Oh that Thou wouldest bless me indeed, and enlarge my coast, and that Thine hand might be with me, and that Thou wouldest keep me from evil, that it may not grieve me! And God granted him that which he requested."

Father we thank you Lord, that like Jabez it is your desire to bless and not harm us. It is your desire to grant us a life of fulfillment and prosperity. It is your good will and pleasure that we reap Kingdom and daily loaded benefits. It is in your mindframe as a Husband to provide, protect and supply all of our needs according

to your glory in Christ Jesus. May we know the truth
of who you are and what you will do on our behalf.
For your word declares but if you ask for bread would
I give you a stone? And if you asked for a fish would I
give you a snake? Even wicked men give their children
desirable things, How much better will your heavenly
Father give? We Thank you that as your children you
give us good things because everything perfect comes
from above. In Jesus Name, Amen.

2. Establish the works of our hands: Psalm 90:17

May the favor of the Lord our God rest on us; establish
the work of our hands for us—yes, establish the work
of our hands.

Father In the name of Jesus, we come before you today
to petition you as the great judge to establish us in our
lands. To establish the works of our hands. To guide and
counsel us with strategies, inventions, dreams, witty
ideas, divine inventions and heavenly blessings. That
whatever we do we do it wholeheartedly as unto the
Lord. Therefore you will prosper the works we give

unto you. May we produce much fruit, may we be rich and have no sorrow, may our lines fall in wealthy places and our pastures become green. May our deserts become streams and our valleys lead us unto mountain tops. May our blessings benefit not only our own families but our communities, people in our reach and cities, states and regions. May we be known in the land for godliness, integrity, upright living, freedom and righteousness. Let our barns be overflowing and our vats full to the brim. May we never lack fresh vision and oil to sustain us in all our doings. In Jesus name, Amen.

3. Prayer to sacrifice: Malachi 3:10

Bring all the tithes into the storehouse, That there may be food in My house, And try Me now in this," Says the Lord of hosts, "If I will not open for you the windows of heaven And pour out for you such blessing That there will not be room enough to receive it.

Father in Jesus name, may we look at our blessing and substance and understand it all comes from you. May it move our hearts to give and give freely. That we would prove you in our way of life in every matter. You are able to do exceedingly, abundantly, above all we can think or ask. I pray we would be faithful in our tithes and offerings that you would show us your Kingdom exchange of multiplication. I pray it would increase our faith and over time we would feel comfortable enough to sow thousands and millions if it is our portion. May we see the fullness of our giving and may we never lack fresh bread or substance for our families through our generosity. May we seek to meet all the needs of your house first because we know in doing this you will supply all of our needs in return. We Thank you King for your majesty, splendor and authority and we bless you. In Jesus' name, Amen.

4. A Prayer for a great harvest: Galatians 6:9

"Let us not become weary in doing good, for at the proper time we will reap a harvest if we do not give up."

Lord, you said you would quicken our mortal bodies with the anointing to stand and see the salvation of the Lord thy God. When we have done all else we stand. Lord let us have the strength, courage, guidance, substance, fight, drive and capability in Christ Jesus to go the distance to see our harvest unfold. We thank you because with God all things are possible. Apart from him we can do nothing. May the fruit we yield be a testimony to all who encounter our lives and may your glory be on display time and time again of what you are able to do when we colabor alongside you. Your thoughts are not our thoughts and ways are not our ways. May we walk in divine timing, peace, rest and FAITH that you have it all under control even when it looks dark and dim. We ask for more understanding in truth and spirit. In Jesus' name, Amen.

CPSIA information can be obtained
at www.ICGtesting.com
Printed in the USA
LVHW040222310322
714849LV00013B/499

9 781662 838774